COOKING THROUGHOUT AMERICAN HISTORY™

What Was Cooking in Julia Grant's White House?

Tanya Larkin

The Rosen Publishing Group's
PowerKids Press™
New York

The recipes in this cookbook are intended for a child to make together with an adult.

Many thanks to Ruth Rosen and her test kitchen.

Published in 2001 by The Rosen Publishing Group, Inc.
29 East 21st Street, New York, NY 10010

First Edition

Book Design: Danielle Primiceri
Layout Design: Emily Muschinske

Photo Credits: pp. 4, 7, 10 © Bettmann/CORBIS; pp. 14, 21 © North Wind Pictures; pp. 9, 13, 17, 19 © Dean Galiano.

Larkin, Tanya.
    What was cooking in Julia Grant's White House? / Tanya Larkin.
        p. cm.— (Cooking throughout American history)
    Includes index.
    Summary: This book describes Julia Dent Grant, wife of the eighteenth president of the United States, her role as first lady, and some of the foods she served at various stages of her life. Includes recipes.
    ISBN 0-8239-5610-5
    1. Cookery, American—Juvenile literature. 2. Grant, Julia Dent, 1806–1902—Juvenile literature. [1. Grant, Julia Dent, 1806–1902. 2. First ladies. 3. Women—Biography. 4. Cookery, American.] I. Title. II. Series.
    2000
    641.3'00973—dc21

Manufactured in the United States of America

Contents

The Promise of Peace

Julia Dent Grant was the wife of General Ulysses Grant. Ulysses became the 18th president of the United States in 1869. President Grant served for two **terms**, from 1869 to 1877. Julia and Ulysses Grant were one of the most popular "first couples." Ulysses Grant gained popularity with the American public after becoming a Civil War hero. He had led the northern states to victory and treated the defeated South with compassion. General Grant won the presidency with the **slogan** "Let us have peace." The Grants promised to bring together the divided nation. Julia grew up on a southern **plantation** near St. Louis, Missouri. Ulysses was a northerner. He was the son of a farmer and had lived in Ohio and Illinois. Their strong union as husband and wife represented the coming together of the North and the South.

◀ *This is a photograph of Julia Grant. She and her husband Ulysses Grant were among the most popular couples in the White House.*

A Loving Union

Julia Grant's brother Fredrick was Ulysses's roommate at West Point Military Academy. Ulysses asked Julia to marry him soon after he met her. While crossing a rickety bridge in a carriage, Julia clung to Ulysses in fear. Ulysses turned to her and said, "How would you like to cling to me for the rest of your life?" After their marriage, she left her family's mansion in Missouri. Julia faithfully followed her "Ulys," as she called him, wherever the United States Army decided to place him. The life of an army wife was a step down from her comfortable life as a wealthy young southern woman. Soldiers were paid low **wages**. Julia, however, stuck by her husband. Although they had very little money, Julia kept her family together. She believed that Ulysses was meant for great things.

This photo shows Julia (left), Ulysses (middle), and Julia's brother Fredrick (right). Julia's brother introduced her to Ulysses many years before. ▶

An Army Wife

Julia had endured years of hardship as an army wife. Military life had taught her how to feed her family with simple, but tasty food. Being an army wife had also prepared Julia for the White House. She had learned how to manage a busy schedule and how to be an energetic hostess. Ulysses quickly moved up the military ladder until he became a general. As a general's wife, Julia was expected to entertain the wives of officers. She hosted a dinner party each time a new officer and his family arrived at the military **posts**. Ulysses was elected president in 1869. Julia was relieved that she didn't have to lead a dull, military life anymore. She felt that she had earned her position as first lady.

Fried Tomatoes

3 tablespoons (44 ml)
   vegetable oil
2 large, green or firm red
   tomatoes
½ cup (118 ml) milk
1 cup (237 ml) flour
Salt
Pepper

HOW TO DO IT:

☞ Slice tomatoes ½ inch (1.3 cm) thick.

☞ Pour milk into a shallow bowl.

☞ Dip tomato slices into the milk.

☞ Dip tomato slices into flour and coat completely.

☞ Heat vegetable oil in a nonstick frying pan.

☞ When the oil is hot, add tomato slices.

☞ Fry tomatoes over a medium low heat.

☞ Carefully turn, so that each side is browned.

☞ Add salt and pepper to taste.

☞ Remove and place on a paper towel to blot oil.

☞ Serves 2.

As a military wife, Julia Grant served her family simple, but tasty meals. She might have served fried tomatoes.

A Close Family of Young and Old

Julia and Ulysses moved into the White House with their 10-year-old son Jessie, their 15-year-old daughter Nellie, and their grandfather Dent, Julia's father. Their two older sons, Fred and Ulysses, Jr. spent most of their time away at college. Ulysses's father, Grandfather Grant, lived nearby and visited often. Julia Grant was a good **homemaker**. Every morning she visited the White House kitchens and **pantries**. She stopped to talk to the people who worked there. She helped them make plans for the day.

◀ *This is a photo of President Ulysses Grant and his wife Julia with their children and grandchildren.*

Family Meals

Julia and Ulysses enjoyed being with their family. When the older Grant boys came home from college, everyone gathered in their parents' bedroom at the end of the day. They spent time telling stories and teasing each other. Ulysses and Jessie, their youngest son, also liked to spend evenings on the White House roof looking at stars through a telescope. Ulysses Grant demanded that his children arrive at meals on time. Once they arrived, he relaxed and played with them. He even started food fights by launching balled-up bread at Nellie and Jessie. Breakfast was the president's favorite meal. During the war, he had cucumbers in vinegar and a cup of coffee for breakfast. When he became president, he developed a taste for a big breakfast. He would eat Spanish mackerel, steak, bacon, fried apples, and pancakes.

Apple Pancakes and Ham

You will need:

1½ cups (355 ml) flour
2½ teaspoons (12 ml)
    baking powder
1 tablespoon (15 ml) sugar
1 teaspoon (5 ml)
    cinnamon
¾ teaspoon (9 ml) salt
1 egg
1 cup milk (237 ml)
3 tablespoons (44 ml)
    vegetable oil
1 cup (237 ml) peeled,
    diced apples
Ham slices
Syrup or honey

HOW TO DO IT:

☞ Sift together flour, baking powder, sugar, cinnamon, and salt.

☞ Mix egg, milk, and vegetable oil.

☞ Combine egg-milk-oil mixture to dry ingredients.

☞ Add apples

☞ Stir just to blend.

☞ (Add a bit more milk to make thinner pancakes.)

☞ Pour pancakes, about ⅓ cup (79 ml), onto a heated griddle or nonstick frying pan.

☞ Turn pancakes to brown on each side.

☞ Serve with ham slices, and syrup or honey.

☞ Makes about a dozen pancakes.

Everyone Was Welcome

Julia and Ulysses invited everyone to visit them at the White House. Julia had only two rules for guests. Everyone had to leave a card with his or her name and address. She wanted to keep track of who came and went. She also wanted all the women to wear hats when they came to visit. Julia held an afternoon party for women each week from 2:00 to 5:00 in the afternoon. The president held more formal evening meetings once a week. Julia felt proud that rich and poor and people of every color were able to "rub elbows" in her home. At one New Year's party, a guest noticed that every type of person was welcome there, from a poor, blind beggar to a wealthy banker.

The Grants opened the White House to everyone for their New Year's Day and Fourth of July parties.

From Mess Hall Cook to Melah

Ulysses brought a **quartermaster** from the army to the White House to serve as cook. The quartermaster treated the White House dining room as if it were a giant **mess hall** for soldiers. He was more interested in the quantity of food than the quality. Julia got tired of eating plain food. She fired the quartermaster. She hired an Italian **gourmet** chef named Melah. Julia's new chef liked to show off by serving 29-course dinners to White House guests. He also changed Ulysses's favorite dishes into gourmet meals. Melah improved upon Ulysses's favorite rice pudding. Ulysses liked his meat very well done. Melah even created a dish that included "almost burnt" steak.

Baked Cheese Hominy Grits

You will need:

2 cups (473 ml) cooked
  hominy grits
⅔ cup (158 ml) milk
3 tablespoons (44 ml)
  melted butter
1½ cup (355 ml) cheddar
  cheese, cut into cubes

HOW TO DO IT:

☞ Have an adult preheat oven to 350 degrees Fahrenheit (177° C)

☞ Combine all ingredients.

☞ Pour into a buttered, shallow quart (liter) baking dish.

☞ Have an adult help you place this pan into a larger baking pan filled with hot water.

☞ Place grits in the oven.

☞ Bake for 1 hour.

☞ Serves 6.

The Grants enjoyed hominy grits as a side dish with their dinner.

Nellie's Wedding

Julia could not have been happier with Melah as her chef. Melah and Julia both liked fancy and expensive entertaining. In 1874, the Grants' daughter married a young Englishman. Julia organized the perfect wedding for Nellie. She had the dining rooms decorated to look like **tropical** jungles. Ferns and potted plants took up every bit of free space. Red roses hung from overhead. A wedding bell made of white roses hung from the ceiling. Melah served a very fancy meal that included soft-shell crabs, lamb, beef, wild duck, and chicken. The menus were covered in white satin. Each person was given a small box of wedding cake tied with white ribbon. The box was a **memento** of the occasion.

Petits Fours and Butter Glaze Frosting

You will need:

1 package of white or
    yellow cake mix
4 tablespoons (59 ml)
    butter
4 cups (946 ml)
    confectioners' sugar
½ cup (118 ml)
    evaporated milk
Food coloring in a tube

HOW TO DO IT:

☞ Prepare the cake mix according to package directions.
☞ Bake in a square cake pan.
☞ When cool, slice cake into small square, diamond, or round shapes.

For the Glaze

☞ Heat butter in a saucepan until it becomes light brown.
☞ Remove from heat.
☞ Add confectioners' sugar and milk.
☞ Stir until well blended.
☞ Pour over cut cake.
☞ Squeeze food coloring from tubes to decorate each cake.

Petits fours are small cakes, usually cut into pretty shapes. They are often served at weddings.

A Tearful Goodbye

Ulysses Grant's second term ended in 1877. Julia pleaded with her husband to run for a third term. Julia had enjoyed being first lady. She also hated the idea of leaving the comfort of the White House. After years of moving from one place to another, the White House had become the closest thing to a permanent home the Grants had known. There had been **scandals** among some of the people that Ulysses had appointed to work for him. This is partly why he secretly decided not to run. He knew that his wife would get angry with him. He was right. Julia burst into tears as they rode away from the White House for the last time. Ulysses comforted his wife by taking her on a trip around the world.

Julia Grant felt that her life as first lady was like "a bright and beautiful dream." ▶

The Penniless Last Days

Ulysses and Julia returned from their trip around the world and found that they were deeply in **debt**. One reason is that they had spent too much money on entertainment over the years. Ulysses tried to save money by returning to his careful, military habits. He even started eating cucumbers in vinegar for breakfast again. When Ulysses became very ill, he forced himself to write his **memoirs**. He hoped that sales from his book would support his family after he died. In 1885, he died at the age of 63. Julia lived on for many years. She also wrote her memoirs. She was the first president's wife to do this. She died in 1902 at the age of 76. Julia Grant once said that her life as first lady was like "a bright and beautiful dream."

Glossary

debt (DEHT) To owe other people money.

gourmet (GOR-may) A person who enjoys food.

homemaker (HOM-may-kur) A person who manages a home.

memento (muh-MEN-toh) Something that serves as a reminder of people or events.

memoirs (MEM-wahrz) Books or letters about personal experiences.

mess hall (MES HOL) A dining room where food is served to soldiers.

pantries (PAN-treez) A closet used for storing food.

plantation (PLAN-tay-shun) A very large farm.

posts (POHSTS) Places where soldiers serve in the military.

quartermaster (KWOR-ter-mas-ter) An army officer who provides food, clothing, and other items for soldiers.

scandals (SKAN-dulz) Improper behavior, especially among elected officials.

slogan (SLOH-gun) A word or phrase used in politics or advertising to sell an idea or a goal.

terms (TURMZ) The limit of time one can be in office.

tropical (TRAH-pih-kul) An area that is very hot and humid.

wages (WAYJ-ez) The money that people earn when they work.

Index

Web Sites

To learn more about Julia Grant, check out these Web sites:
http://www.whitehouse.gov/WH/glimpse/firstladies/html/jg18.html
http://www.americanpresidents.com/jgrant.html